Originally published in Japanese under the title *Docchikana?* by Child Honsha Co. Ltd., Tokyo.
English translation rights arranged with Child Honsha Co. Ltd., through Japan Foreign-Rights Centre.

Kids Can Press acknowledges the financial support of the Government of Ontario, through the Ontario Media Development Corporation's Ontario Book Initiative; the Ontario Arts Council; the Canada Council for the Arts; and the Government of Canada, through the CBF, for our publishing activity.

Published in Canada by
Kids Can Press Ltd.
25 Dockside Drive
Toronto, ON M5A 0B5

Published in the U.S. by
Kids Can Press Ltd.
2250 Military Road
Tonawanda, NY 14150

www.kidscanpress.com

English edition edited by Yvette Ghione

This book is smyth sewn casebound.

Manufactured in Shenzen, China, in 10/2012 by C & C Offset Printing Co.

CM 13 0 9 8 7 6 5 4 3 2 1

Library and Archives Canada Cataloguing in Publication

Mamada, Mineko, 1952–

Which is round? Which is bigger? / Mineko Mamada.

Translation of: Docchikana?
For ages 2–6.

ISBN 978-1-55453-973-4

1. Shapes — Juvenile literature. 2. Size judgment — Juvenile literature.
3. Picture books for children. I. Title.

QA445.5.M3413 2013   j516'.15   C2012-906241-3

Kids Can Press is a **lorus**™ Entertainment company

Which Is Round?
Which Is Bigger?

Mineko Mamada

Kids Can Press

Which one is round?

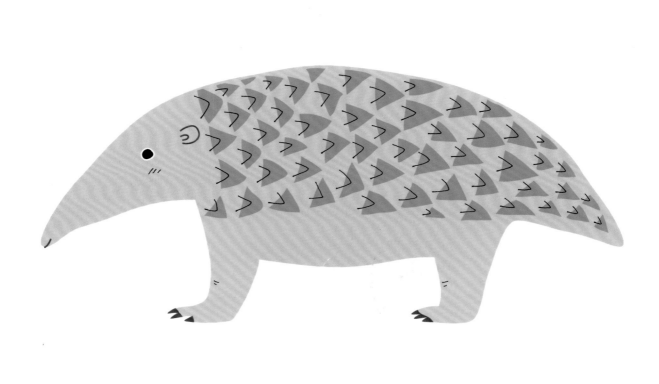

Which one is round?
What do you think?

Which one is bigger?

Which one is bigger?
What do you think?

Which one is longer?

Which one is longer?
What do you think?

Which one is faster?

Which one is faster?
What do you think?

Which one is higher?

Which one is higher?
What do you think?

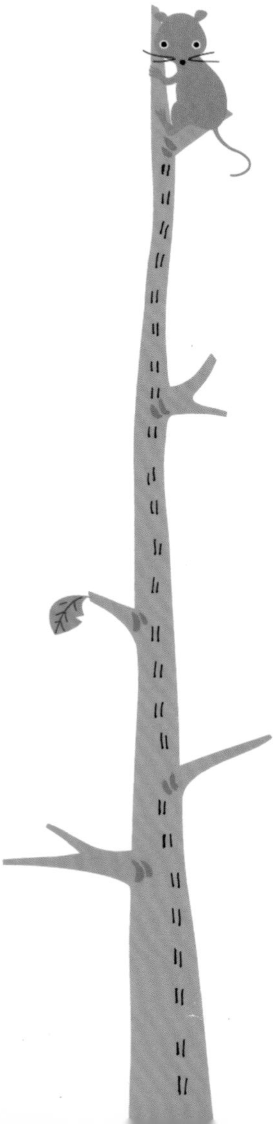

Which one is red?

Which one is red?
What do you think?

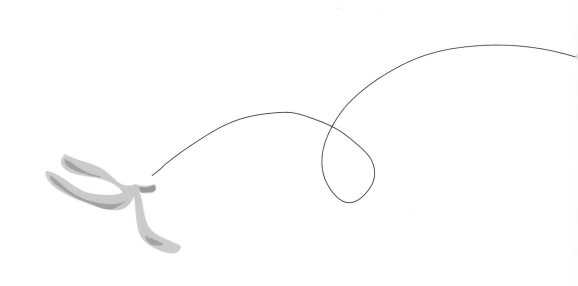